Dearly, Nearly, Insincerely

What Is an Adverb?

To Elio, Gina, and Vince who get
along swimmingly   —B.P.C.

For Sari   —B.G.

Dearly, Nearly, Insincerely

What Is an Adverb?

by Brian P. Cleary

illustrated by Brian Gable

 CAROLRHODA BOOKS, INC. / MINNEAPOLIS

AdVerbs add character, sizzle, and fizz

To your phrase or your sentence, whatever it is!

Frankly, this hot dog just couldn't be better.

Sheepishly, Fred found he'd ruined his sweater.

If they tell us **how**, they're an "adVerb of manner,"

Like, slowly this summer, my sister got tanner.

"Frequency adverbs" will tell us **how often**,

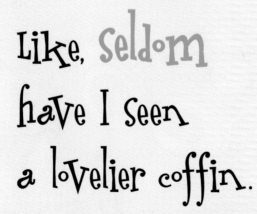

Like, seldom have I seen a lovelier coffin.

Always eat cookies,
and never eat pine.

Sometimes I'm nervous,
but usually fine.

They give us a time,
a place, and
a number,

Like, yesterday, over there,
I was in slumber.

First, I was tired,

then, I was woozy,

Next, I began feeling sleepy and snoozy.

They modify **adVerbs,** like, she sang quite nicely.

Or he speaks so swiftly but Very precisely.

Presently, pleasantly, properly praise.

Speedily, sometimes quite greedily, graze.

Bitterly angry, bitingly cold,

Brilliantly burgundy, shockingly old.

The adjective's "good,"
the **adverb** is "well."

So now that
you know that,
you're able to tell

That Well's how you felt,
and good was your day.

Yes, Well is a
Very deep Subject,
I'd Say!

Truly, deeply,
sadly, badly—

TRULY

DEEPLY

SADLY

BADLY

I tell you these are
adverbs, gladly.

So, what is an **adVerb?**

Do you know?

About the Author & Illustrator

BRIAN P. CLEARY is the author of several other picture books, including <u>A Mink, a Fink, a Skating Rink: What Is a Noun?</u>, <u>To Root, to Toot, to Parachute: What Is a Verb?</u>, <u>Hairy, Scary, Ordinary: What Is an Adjective?</u>, and <u>Under, Over, By the Clover: What Is a Preposition?</u>

BRIAN GABLE is the illustrator of <u>Under, Over, By the Clover: What Is a Preposition?</u> He lives in Toronto, Ontario, where he works as a political cartoonist.

Text copyright © 2003 by Brian P. Cleary
Illustrations copyright © 2003 by Brian Gable

Carolrhoda Books, Inc., a division of Lerner Publishing Group
241 First Avenue North, Minneapolis, MN 55401 U.S.A.

Website address: www.lernerbooks.com

Library of Congress Cataloging-in-Publication Data

Cleary, Brian P., 1959—
    Dearly, nearly, insincerely : what is an adverb? / by Brian P. Cleary;
    illustrated by Brian Gable.
       p.   cm. — (Words are categorical)
    Summary: Rhyming text and illustrations present numerous examples of
adverbs and their functions.
    ISBN: 0—87614—924—7 (lib. bdg. : alk. paper)
    1. English language—Adverb—Juvenile literature. [1. English language—
Adverb.] I. Gable, Brian, 1949— II. Title.
PE1325 .C57 2003
428.2—dc21   2002003012

Manufactured in the United States of America
  3 4 5 6 — JR — 08 07 06 05 04